DECOY

DECOY

POEMS BY ELAINE EQUI

COFFEE HOUSE PRESS :: MINNEAPOLIS

Some of these poems have appeared in *Abacus, American Letters & Commentary, The American Poetry Review, The American Voice, The Archive Newsletter, B City, Caliban, Chelsea, Conjunctions, Epoch, Furnitures, Gas, Hot Bird MFG, Lacanian Ink, Long News: In The Short Century, New American Writing, No Roses Review, St. Mark's Poetry Project Newsletter, Sulfur, XXIst Century*, and *The World*.

The publishers would like to thank the following funders for assistance that helped make this book possible: National Endowment for the Arts, a federal agency; The Jerome Foundation; The Lannan Foundation; The Andrew W. Mellon Foundation; and the McKnight Foundation. This activity is made possible in part by a grant provided by the Minnesota State Arts Board, through an appropriation by the Minnesota State Legislature. Major new marketing initiatives have been made possible by the Lila Wallace-Reader's Digest Literary Publishers Marketing Development Program, funded through a grant to the Council of Literary Magazines and Presses.

Coffee House Press books are available to the trade through our primary distributor, Consortium Book Sales & Distribution, 1045 Westgate Drive, Saint Paul, MN 55114. Our books are also available through all major library distributors and jobbers, and through most small press distributors, including Bookpeople, Inland, and Small Press Distribution. For personal orders, catalogs or other information, write to: Coffee House Press
27 North Fourth Street, Suite 400, Minneapolis, MN 55401

Library of Congress CIP data
Equi, Elaine.
  Decoy / by Elaine Equi.
    p.   cm.
  ISBN 1-56689-026-8 (paperback : acid-free)
    I. Title.
PS3555.Q5D43 1994
811'.54—dc20   94-12603
                                                          CIP

10 9 8 7 6 5 4 3 2 1

TABLE OF CONTENTS

PART I

PART II

PART III

PART IV

for Jerome Sala

PART I

BRAND X

I know you think
this is about sex
but that's only because
it's really about advertising.

Someone talking
in an office.
Someone comparing two things.

I make decisions
or my body
makes them for me
and certain nights
everything is perfect.

Wedges of light flap
slow as Indian summer.
A red receding.

There is real violence
but it's an after-dinner violence
mellow in the air
as sex is a kind of violence

like anything
that pulls us toward it
even though we're unable
to ask for it by name.

All writing is a form
of transvestism.

Men in camisoles.
Women drinking port
and smoking thin cigars.

Think of Flaubert, Proust
Mallarmé in drag.

Or a woman (any woman)
trying on a man's power:
"Now I clothe myself
in your blood, your wars."

Like getting dressed
in a warm room
on a cold day

the sly smile
of the self
as it goes to sleep.

Everything contained within.
You read Rilke
and you become Rilke.

Nothing can stop this
endless, transformative
flow of selves
        (our)selves
into other, opposite,
even objects and animals.

In a dream I took my
blue pentagram shirt
to the cleaners

and they said
it would take
three whole months
to get the werewolf out!

DEAR MICHAEL

The real
is looser
than the hyper-real

and I'm glad
after all these years
to tell them apart.

Fairfield Porter says:
"I don't paint space,
I paint the air"

and I say
I don't look at color
(at least in your backyard)
I breathe it.

Not that you
remind me of Fairfield Porter
(to bring up class!)

it's just that
I was so happy
to be in your guest room
reading Barbara Guest

with "real" bluebirds outside
and Hank Williams warbling
in the next room.

Domesticity,
that's what my dream
was about

as in: where's the tea,
the cups, the sign
over the sink that reads

"There is a silent
meaning behind everything"

(like in a monastery)

and when people ask
we tell them that you're
going through a Thomas Merton phase

but still like to party
on weekends.

IN THE MAIL TODAY

1.

A reminder
that my student loan
is overdue.

Amazing, this debt
from another life
when I waitressed
and read 19th-century novels.

First the French.
Then the British.

Now, forty
and still paying.

2.

A long letter
from a new friend
in Minnesota
where it's even colder
than it is here—
2 below to our 18 degrees.

It ends:

I feel almost
as if I should
apologize

for dumping
all these words
on you.

Strange—
we speak this way,
humans do,
so seldom now
that it almost seems
on the outside.

3.

A postcard
from Joe Brainard.

Dear Elaine and Jerome,
         Don't miss Ruby Stone's
(she's a he) cooking show
Come and Get It on Saturdays
at 1:00 P.M. on channel 17.

4.

An envelope
from St. Anthony's
(patron of lost things)
Church.

Ornately addressed
to me but with
nothing inside,

the message
apparently forgotten
or misplaced.

AFTER HERRICK

true calendars
tell ripe
each change

assuage
as night does

doting
and yet shines

enclosed in
rhymes
sphering

Bestrewed
with Ovid
(bellman Ovid)

words
for meat
give melody
over rocks

reading
by degrees

rivers
turn awhile
to men

awhile
they glide
full of meaning

shearing
melody's
meeting

DESTINATIONS

1.

A hand
leafs through
autumn

with a logic
that shines
like oxblood.

Every morning
I don't hear it

the absence
behind the bird.

Nudging the frame.
Singing its head off.

2.

Your letter
is full of energy

as though you were
inside a color
a whole flock of them

but I slept
on the day
I was born

and see sleep
as others see the world.

A lamp filled with
the oil of dreams

hisses, stone chatter.

3.

In brine daylight
thought becomes brimmed.
Fraught with sudden,
steeped in listening.

The jars
around which presence
gathers its virtues.

To inhabit my walk
(though a pleasure)
and all that that conveys

(limitations, frames).

This romance
of going from city to city
with a lamp.

Troll-like
. . . in tufts

something other
than silence
surrounds my words.

To follow
unwillingly

with belly
and lip
thrust out,

to follow
the unwilling

through the silence
of the room

and the silence
of the page

(mere conventions)

as if language existed
"a dis-figured voice"
outside the body

to be poured
from one container
into another

—the illusion of it!

GHOST TEXT

When I talk
to the spirits
on the spirit-phone

it becomes choreography

            "all a trick"

waltzing, demure

but she (other/mother)
howls
from the depths
of her bones

with genuine respect
for those that live
inside the body

inside the poem

the whiteness
around the words

that also wants to speak

DREADLOCKS

for Jean Michel Basquiat

A last look
in the rearview mirror
and it's over.

All the colors
wired together
so when he
combs his hair
the train explodes.

ART ABOUT FEAR

I.

Be careful with that book.
It's not a book. It's a person

and it changes. See, there's lavender
under the frost. And an accident.

Grow up and decide for yourself
what it's about, but it's too bad

it can't be me because I'm very good
if you're terrified. That's what I do.

Art about fear. Girls that burst
into flames while getting a suntan.

2.

Text
is something
we all must
share

the burden of
carrying.

Rub shoulders with
and give it a push.

Evening's door
swings open
and there you are
in my skyline
with the peek-a-boo crotch.

Body dimensions sweep.
I'm sweeping.

Wrong in this context
but I can imagine another
where suppose . . .

3.

His offering me a cigarette
only seemed to underscore
the close-but-no-cigar bit.

When I perceive an obstacle
I feel it physically.
How approach? How get past?

Its looming legend.
Pepper trees that can walk
two full miles per day.

The question isn't
whether it's true or not
but whether you *want* to believe it.

4.

Some objects
are like a sieve
that language
passes through
while others
repel the alphabet
with a harsh
clanging skin.
Minor intelligences
perched on
the tip of.
Go ahead, say it
in your Bullwinkle French.

5.

You know classical perspective doesn't really
exist, but off in your vortex, it sounds roman-
tic. Seeping through those flickering inhibitions
that lead back home to maroon with its old-
fashioned horror. Like hair standing on end,
the water shot straight up out of the fountain.
This was my first painting. The portrait of a
lonely, intrepid rationalist besieged by spirits.

6.

Eventually meaning
does arrive.
The latecomer
with a festive air.

As if to say:
"There are paintings.
There are books, but nothing
here to frighten you."

Then suddenly
and for no reason
it disappears again.

What recourse
against such loss
but to make a list.

Say prayers.
Wash clothes.
Buy groceries.
Call David.

7.

After the funeral
we threw open the windows.

Cooling there.
Words,
loaves of them.

Such a lonely sound.
A carriage
(in these modern times)
passing below.

With Rimbaud
and his mistress
stuck inside.

Still searching
for that spider
that goes so fast
and travels far.

Its poisonous scratches
like those of a pen.

PART II

TO PAUL CELAN

Smooth out
the ragged darkness
with a sprawling hand

even so
we can't read
its life-line

only follow
your disappearance
into this make-believe place

where you leave us
distracted by a fox-colored
and a grape-colored

and the uneasy sensation
of something moving,
burrowing beneath.

Sound calls forth
but union is wordless.
Attachments' arms poke through.
Breaks rested in: bring it here.
"Bring it on home."
Pinpoints on the cusp of
clumsy. Now look, you've
unscrewed the whole thing.
Administering or administrating?
To straighten glints raw honey.
The mythology that sets in motion.

SEEMS/BECOMES

nightlights
fleece in braille

past some platonic
suburb

to look into
the zero pond

a peg whistle
half heart
with window

brooding
until there's
no other way

and you just have to
stick out your neck
and follow it

As if there were ways
to make shame palatable,
tasseled and excruciating

the fantasy furniture
of a thousand and one
claustrophobic afternoons.

Father in his
leopard jockstrap.

Mother in her
leopard sarong.

And me on the chaise longue
glum in the midst of all glamour.

Time passes
but I grow no older—

all the genitalia
of my youth
kept like musical instruments
that play themselves.

Strange and atonal

night in the middle of day
day in the middle of night

clouds reflected
in a heart-shaped pool.

"I've just gotten
to the point where
I can deal with roaches

but mice—

mice are still
beyond me."

SQUARE DANCE

Light circles
duck gray buildings.

Boxy configurations
that give one
a "municipal" feeling

that one's money
is safe
that one's secrets
are safe

locked away from
distracting breezes
which may carry off
on a whim

all that our parents
worked so hard to acquire.

The idea of one idea
added to another,

of carrying "someone
else's baby."

Ascending the stairs
we know that power
and money are not rational

and yet there is
something so charming
about the architecture
of these ideas

that people still
step lightly so as
not to disturb the system.

How often
in the middle
of the night

have I longed
for your temperance
like a stretch of
out-in-the-open sleep.

Unencumbered by
strange carvings/cravings,

the body grown
almost transparent.

By day, a scavenger
staring at an array
of choices—

bold colors, attractive design.

Unlike those people
who carry "real food" home,
moving so effortlessly.

It is illusion
that weighs
a person down.

He sits between the phone and the refrigerator.
While behind him, the trees outside the window
are caked with snow. Everything is silent, but
at a slightly different pitch, and he sits like
one lost in the Bermuda Triangle of their various
stillnesses. To his right is a glass of vodka.
To his left, hovering just above the shoulder,
is a large mysterious ball of light. Clearly,
it frightens him, but still he looks, with eyes
that are both liquid and resigned, as if he
always expected this to happen. Months
earlier, his wife asked for a divorce.
Months later will find him in the hospital
after a stroke. Yet at just this moment, nothing
seems to matter except that he listen to whatever
has traveled light-years to reach him—a sound
small as the ice melting in his glass.

Today is woven
out of a marvelous
synthetic fabric
which we have
not discovered
and have no name for.
Light, cool, porous
like skin, only transparent.
I remember when
I used to think love
meant being surrounded
by plastic hula-girls
and wind-up poodles
in a place where
nothing was real
except our feelings.
The obvious authenticity
of them—why was it
so important?

have three things in common: bedwetting
past the age of twelve, several episodes
of starting fires, torturing animals.
When I close my eyes at the end of the day,
this is all that comes to mind. After washing
dishes, grading papers, writing letters, long
conversations on the phone and in restaurants,
time spent memorizing Italian verbs: *cogliere*
to gather, *accendere* to light—nothing else
it turns out is quite so memorable to me as this.
The sort of thing you hear once and, for some reason,
take it with to your grave. Strange, how we mark
our place in the world.

It's the kind of street
that would be behind
one of those crooners
who sang on TV in the 1950s.

A streetlamp, a cemetery
and a big full moon.
What more could a person
want or need?

O to live on nothing
but arugula and espresso,
forever doing penance
in that somber church
across the street.

The one that's surrounded
by a wall that leans on you
as much as you lean on it.

The one full of flickering lights
and statues that talk.
"The dead," they say.
"The dead will outlive us all."

STATUS QUO

For a long time
you existed
before we came
to celebrate
your self-
sufficiency or
to love your indifference
with its unlatched
murmuring, and it
is only stubbornness
that makes things
wish to resemble
themselves. Twisting
away from this
I am out the door
of my mouth
for a heart's apéritif.
Its untenanted and
untenable narratives
I distrust and that
is their value
frayed and phrased
in layers.

THIS IS NOT A POEM

the poem exists
always and only
in the mind
of the reader

and these words
can never be more than
arrows, breadcrumbs

a map of abbreviations
however crude or elaborate

the poem comes into being
as the writer reads
and the reader anticipates

one can fill every inch
with writing and still
be no closer to the poem

as it lies there
a liar with a beautiful voice
that is often mistaken for silence

PART III

PRESCRIPTION

Take Herrick
for melancholy

Niedecker
for clarity

O'Hara
for nerve

It started badly. Tossed out of
the cart's lap for having too many
loopholes. She wore her nuance
like a noose to ruffle clarity.
The sad beginnings and endings
affixed to. Mimed briefly, then
leveled—though this was just
the tip of the thawing. "Ah, woman,
that irony which makes community
impossible." Cut down the middle of
gender's root. The buzz of was. Its
foliage intoned.

MOONLIGHT ON LOBSTER

bars on windows
cannot deter

its classical
sense of self
from streaming through

like acquisition
at an auction

that flesh
whose meat
is mostly ephemera

transcribing

they had strawberries
and linen napkins too

A LEMON

In the lemon
we find a fire
that cools, coos.
Mathematically succinct
it is a flame
which unlike most
can be cut in half
or thirds if you prefer.
In the skin
of its lantern
light implodes,
slowing to the speed
of mere human endeavor
before giving itself
in a last sudden burst
like eyesight
to the blindness
of the mouth.

READING AKHMATOVA

Sick and reading Akhmatova.
All afternoon
cups of tea

then into the larger teacup
of a hot tub.

Half of me
feels ethereal
while the other half wonders

was it really possible
she spent that much time
falling in and out of love?

Somehow the aftertaste
of her words
makes me think
it was more a career choice

and that the bitter
medicine of her poems

is directed
not toward the lover
but rather the reader

who forces her to reenact
the same scene
saying over and over

"you are the one"
"you are the one"
"you are the one."

There is a point when mourning becomes
luxurious. Deeply inhaled like a cigarette,
sadness settles on the skin. Never to ———,
O never again. The windows are boarded up
with art, but real wind blows through the
paintings. Blows at times from the inside out.
Stale as old clothes, old smoke, here comes
the grief in tiny puffs. Mine, but belonging
to others too.

POEM

Like a window
open in winter

I look to the edge of
hair, teeth, nails.

Too busy to be internal
libido calmly rushes

in one orchard
and out another.

Its knotted weather
spreads brightly.

Its peach thread melody
is squandered away.

PERMISSION

the beauty of it
is not static
but pierced

like birdsong
with a series
of pauses

aspiring to waver
between giving
and taking
for as long as possible

DECOY

violins
scissor a tune
streaked with animal

not where I want to be
but where I am

(makes the connection)

oh yes, now I recognize it

vigilantly
mapped out

facts awaken
almost by touch

a shape
unseen
yet so familiar

*

there was an old uncle vampire
giving his niece a drink

but it was the shabbiness
of where it took place
(not in a Gothic drawing room)
that upset us

*

think of ready-ing
as doing the prerequisite reading

clouds slide
smoothly over the skin

"He lives in his legend
and that's about it"

a neatly folded labyrinth

going by:
blue blooms on the red field
of a dress in motion

if only we could get
that feeling back where
it's the landscape that moves
and the viewer who stands still

"Yes, yes
we have to get together

and no, I don't
remember who you are."

*

somewhere behind eye and ear
coffee is brewing, bread baking

the sign reads:
"Looks are deceiving
it's eating
that is believing—

YOU WERE BORN TO EAT"

mind crawls like a fly
over the painted fruit

form struggles
not only to emerge
but also to sink
back into matter

these flowers
smell more dead
than alive

so where does the mania
for containment come from?

*

historically the doppelganger
is not a nice person

bone prism casts
body-stocking shadows

see Artaud in the role
of game-show host

or *Let's Make a Deal*
as theater of cruelty

flames nest
doubling back

dissolves into unrest
and needless hyperbole

an impersonation
pressing down on

*

UFO SLICES HOTEL
CAKE WITH FIRE ESCAPE ICING

willow seen by candlelight
poems read by flashlight

      sage
      marigolds
      Salems
      Rolling Rock

"You're going to hell
in a handbasket with the rest of us"

*

stains:
what works on paper
doesn't always

and that's the story of my life

biting through
glimpses

an exchange of parcel
password, fishbowl, globe

"Most normal people are sick"

until at some point
evil stops being evil
and just stands childishly
under the childish stars

SOUVENIR

These curiosities
bring us back with them
curious as ever.

Backlogs
that open the heart
with the surgery of music

like Apollinaire's
hunting horns
which "die along the wind."

It is an airy enterprise
weaving Provençal flowers
on Elizabethan latticework.

You could say that
any household object
comes to us in the same way

compressing
all of history
into a swizzle stick.

Now out of context
the mermaid never tires
of swimming/speaking
in circles.

PART IV

When our plane goes down
it falls into the future
where already you have stepped
from the wreckage and hailed
us a cab. Looking back, it
turns out to have been only
a toy plane anyway. Bright red,
the debris of which is scattered
like lobster shells on a freshly
cut lawn. I wonder where we are,
but the blonde next to you in the
back seat starts sucking my finger
whenever I point out something
as if to say, "Why bother?" And
in any case, we seem quite at home
wherever we are, so that, getting out
of the cab, I feel for the first time
in a long time, lucky to be alive.
My coat open. My chest bare. My breasts
cold and white in the wind.

SARCOPHAGUS

for
all
that
titillates

for
all
that
is
kind

you
stand
written

as
a
history
of
that
golden
age
of
self

o
singular
monument

representative
of
the
lower

case
lower
caste

stand
and
see
how
in
your
shadow

everything
shrinks
from
your
total
disregard
for
its
power

AFTER BACON

to know the names
of all the muses, planets, plants
(everything that ever existed)

unpronounceable
faded and obscure
Greek and Latin names

and to still find
in this world

a place for them
        to mate
            match with . . .

like a Cinderella
who is herself
made of glass

o empiricism
o anatomy

A H !

How good it feels
even briefly
to stretch
the long neck
of narcissism.
One happiest
blue-checkered tablecloth
of infinite seeing
eye to I.
And with love's mask
in place
what world lies
behind the curtain?
In Rome, it's true
there is no Rome
but elsewhere—plenty.

SO WHAT

Sometimes I wake up alone, she said,
and the idea of audience

is an unnecessary contrivance.
The poem is not here either.

It is, I think, a little to the left
outside the margin. Or perhaps

by the time you read this, it will
have gone further away. It may be

in another bed, just as I dream
of being in my mother's bed

sick and wearing her lipstick
with a child, a daughter,

who hasn't spoken to me in years.
I don't care. I don't miss her.

"Go back to sleep,"
is what I say to my body.

"Take off your clothes,"
is what I say to my mind.

BOTH OF US WRITING

Me in bed
and you at the table.

Both of us
writing

these rooms
this experience—

our marriage
the corridor between.

fire spreads
                fluently

as "babble"

(blush) (undertow)

caught up she says:

"talk to me
talk to me"

a scattering of possible outcomes

then squints a lifetime's
worth of it
                error

as in "what's wrong with
this picture?"

wall: a rippling

world as train station
inside and out

aggression cresting
in games of exchange

innate interiors
to be transcribed
transgressed

when one gives
full force to a whim
the heart is a tightfisted dictator

first smoke
then the kindling
of intention

heat multiplies

what the sky
tastes of the earth
and vice versa

dissonant chimes calling

the already
and the not-yet of it

touched and retouched
by attention's wingspan

circling
a search for outside

as it tests its authority/
ownership within

still, I'm not certain
I want all that drama

to give in
        mends

to win
strikes a blow
or blows like the wind

intimate beyond speech
we see only the "thereness"
of people, objects

margins where colors repeat
making a pattern/
present of the unstable past

now including
now excluding

parenthesis
like a flock of birds

always shifting
and full of cries

LATER

if I disconnect
if I leave it at
          a word

it's only because
everything is already
so much a part
of everything else

and the desire
to say "mine"
or to own

is almost as strong
as the desire to belong
or be owned by

those commercials
and popular songs

ripped from
the genre of kissing

like dragonflies
the headlines buzz

where bewitched
our choices narrow

AGAIN

how tired you look

or how tired
that part of me
that is you looks

come to say hello
or good-bye

TO HARRY CROSBY AT THE
HOTEL DES ARTISTES

In 1979, on the 50th anniversary of your
double-suicide, I came like a bridesmaid
dressed in black to scatter rose petals
in the lobby. Then I went home and listened
to Joy Division, whose lead singer would
also kill himself. Death was everywhere
at the time, though mostly as a fashion
statement—kohl around the eyes and
safety pins through the cheek—with
the real devastation still to come. Now it
is 1993 and no one much likes to glamorize
their death wish, not since AIDS has made
absence so conspicuous. Today people prefer
to look healthy, and it's mineral water I
toast you with in the Art Deco jungle of the
hotel bar. Not the sort of place I'd choose
if I were going to end it all, but if I've
become anything, I hope it's more tolerant—
even of the very rich. Outside on the ground
there is no snow yet, but old rice the color
of ivory, leftover from some other wedding,
and in the bare trees, white lights like a
handful of rice, transformed on this winter
afternoon into "the pleasure of neon in daylight."
Perfect moments in an imperfect world, joined
together so that even death cannot separate them.

Can a poem cast a shadow
or cut through rock?
Clear a path? Uproot
the way a face can
transform a landscape
displace a mind—
the way Jacob followed
an image of Rachel's face
through a fourteen-year maze.
An endless grinding routine
of work and sex, though where
and with whom, all a blur.
All but the glitter of her eyes
in the scythe as it swept
across the fields, which is not
unlike the way I look at your face
and how it moves me endlessly
to meander without purpose,
without certainty, and no way
to reach it but through the poem.

SOMETIMES I GET DISTRACTED

for Philip Whalen

Throwing a ball

like a bridge
over an old wound

like a cape
thrown chivalrously
over incoherent muck.

Catching it
is easy.

"Now toss it back,"

says the Zen monk
standing in his garden
centuries away.

COMPLETE SET

Perennial
white on white
blooms in winter

where all that
is unspecific looms
wooing

turning or torn off

"the inessential"

starling
caught between
the signatures
of two buildings

the fox returning
to the fable's lair

rain at night
and traffic
scattered like leaves.

Is cadence then
the opposite of decadence?

Baudelaire would not think so.